★

FUN & CREATIVE
WORKSHOP ACTIVITIES

COOL

METALWORKING

PROJECTS

REBECCA
FELIX

Checkerboard
Library

An Imprint of Abdo Publishing
abdopublishing.com

ABDOPUBLISHING.COM

Published by Abdo Publishing, a division of ABDO, PO Box 398166, Minneapolis, Minnesota 55439. Copyright © 2017 by Abdo Consulting Group, Inc. International copyrights reserved in all countries. No part of this book may be reproduced in any form without written permission from the publisher. Checkerboard Library™ is a trademark and logo of Abdo Publishing.

Printed in the United States of America, North Mankato, Minnesota
062016
092016

THIS BOOK CONTAINS RECYCLED MATERIALS

Design and Production: Mighty Media, Inc.
Series Editor: Paige V. Polinsky
Photo Credits: Rebecca Felix, Paige V. Polinsky, Shutterstock

The following manufacturers/names appearing in this book are trademarks: J-B® KwikWeld™, Sharpie®

Library of Congress Cataloging-in-Publication Data

Names: Felix, Rebecca, 1984- author.
Title: Cool metalworking projects : fun & creative workshop activities / Rebecca Felix.
Description: Minneapolis, Minnesota : Abdo Publishing, [2017] | Series: Cool industrial arts | Includes index.
Identifiers: LCCN 2016006207 (print) | LCCN 2016010233 (ebook) | ISBN 9781680781298 (print) | ISBN 9781680775495 (ebook)
Subjects: LCSH: Metal-work--Juvenile literature.
Classification: LCC TT205 .F425 2017 (print) | LCC TT205 (ebook) | DDC 684.09--dc23
LC record available at http://lccn.loc.gov/2016006207

TO ADULT HELPERS

This is your chance to help children learn about industrial arts! They will also develop new skills, gain confidence, and make cool things. These activities are designed to teach children how to work with metal. Readers may need more assistance for some activities than others. Be there to offer guidance when they need it. Encourage them to do as much as they can on their own. Be a cheerleader for their creativity!

Look at the beginning of each project for its difficulty rating (EASY, INTERMEDIATE, ADVANCED).

TABLE (OF) CONTENTS

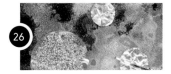

WHAT

IS METALWORKING?

Metalworking is making things out of metal. Furniture, jewelry, tools, and more can be made of metal. Metals are found in nature. They are usually found underground. People first began using metal to create tools thousands of years ago.

METALWORKING TECHNIQUES

Workshop Tips

The main thing a metal workshop needs is a flat, hard work surface. This can be in the garage, in the basement, or at the kitchen table. Just make sure you get **permission**! Then, follow the tips below to work safely.

- Keep your workspace clean and free of clutter. Tools should be within easy reach and stored in safe places.

- Make sure the room is well **ventilated**.

- Wear thick gloves with a rubber coating when handling sharp metal.

- Wear rubber gloves when using spray paint.

- Put a piece of scrap wood or old cutting board on your work surface. Place the metal you're working with on the wood.

Essential Safety Gear

- Gloves
- Safety goggles
- Face mask
- Closed-toe shoes

Be Prepared

- Read the entire project before you begin.
- Make sure you have everything you need to do the project.
- Follow the directions carefully.
- Clean up after you are finished.

ADULT HELPERS

Working with metal can be **dangerous**. Metal pieces can have sharp edges. The tools used to cut and shape metal can also be sharp. That means you should have an adult standing by for some of these projects.

KEY SYMBOLS

In this book, you may see one or more symbols at the beginning of a project. Here is what they mean:

SUPER SHARP!
A sharp tool is needed.
Get help!

GLOVES
Hand protection should be worn for certain steps in this project.

SAFETY GOGGLES
Eye protection should be worn for certain steps in this project.

FACE MASK
Doing this project creates dust or requires glues with strong odors. A face mask should be worn for protection.

TOOLS OF THE TRADE

Here are some of the materials you will need for the projects in this book.

BEARING BALL

BOLTS

CERAMIC DISC MAGNETS

CHENILLE STEMS

COPPER SHEET METAL

DUCT CAPS

FLAT COPPER WIRE

FLEX DUCT SPLICE CONNECTOR COLLAR

GALVANIZED WIRE

HAMMER

HEX NUTS

LARGE NAILS

METAL EXTENSION SPRINGS

METAL GLUE

METAL TIE PLATES

NEEDLE-NOSE PLIERS

SANDPAPER

STEEL GAS VENT TEE CAP

TIN SNIPS

WIRE CUTTERS

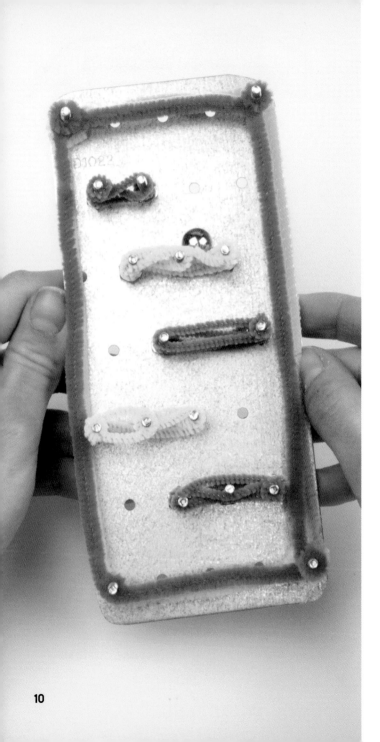

METAL + WIRE
MAZE

GET THE BEARING BALL FROM THE TOP TO THE BOTTOM!

MATERIALS

- tin snips
- metal tie plate, 3⅛" × 7" (7.9 × 17.8 cm)
- 100-grit sandpaper
- 20 #6-32 × 1" (2.5 cm) bolts
- 20 #6-32 hex nuts
- screwdriver (should match the bolts)
- needle-nose pliers
- 9 to 12 chenille stems
- ½" (1.3 cm) bearing ball
- ½" (1.3 cm) ceramic disc magnet

MAKING THE BASE + BORDER

1 Put on safety goggles. Use tin snips to round off the corners of the tie plate. Be careful not to cut too close to the holes.

2 Sand the cut corners until smooth.

3 **Insert** a bolt into each corner hole on the tie plate. Carefully flip the tie plate over. Then screw a hex nut onto each bolt.

Continued on the next page.

11

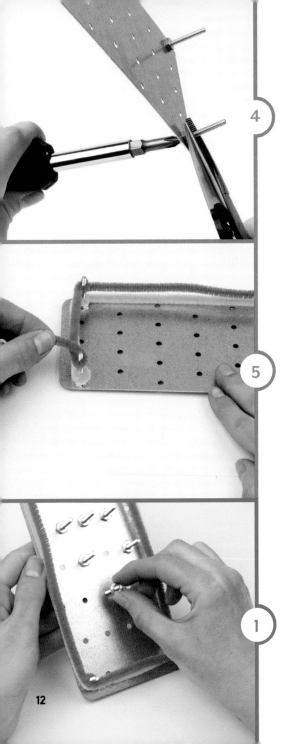

4 Use the screwdriver and pliers to tighten the nuts.

5 Wrap chenille stems around the bolts to form a rectangular border. Make two rows.

MAKING THE MAZE

1 **Insert** bolts into some of the holes inside the maze. Screw a hex nut onto each bolt. Add as many as you like, wherever you like.

2 Tighten the nuts with the screwdriver and pliers.

TIP
It helps to plan your maze first. Sketch ideas on a piece of paper.

3 Wind chenille stems around the inner bolts to create your maze. Some of the stems should touch the border.

4 Place the bearing ball at the top of your maze. Tip the maze back and forth so the ball rolls to the bottom. Did it work? Rewrap wires or move bolts as needed to make the maze work.

5 When not using the maze, set the magnet in a corner of the tie plate. Then set the ball on the magnet. It will stick to the maze!

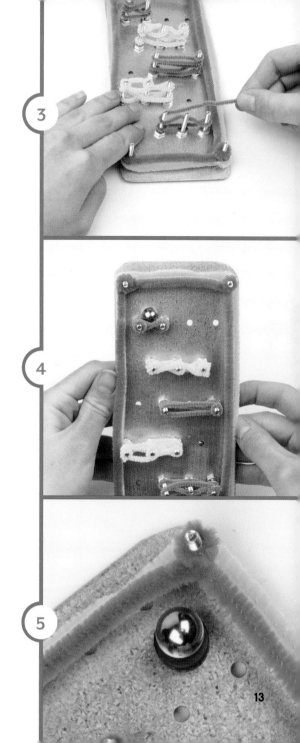

TINY
TIE-PLATE NOTEBOOK

MAKE A MINI METAL NOTEBOOK!

PREPPING THE PAPER

1. Trace a tie plate on a piece of paper five times.

2. **Stack** all the paper. Put the marked sheet on top. Secure the paper with binder clips.

3. Cut the tie-plate shapes out along the lines.

4. Stack the cut pages. Place the tie plate on top of the stack. Draw dots through the holes along one long side.

Continued on the next page.

5 Remove the tie plate and keep the paper **stacked**. Punch holes in the paper over the marked dots.

FINISHING THE COVERS

1 Put on safety goggles. Use tin snips to round off the corners of both tie plates. Be careful not to cut too close to the holes.

2 Sand the cut corners until smooth.

3 Place the paper pages between the two tie plates. Secure the stack with binder clips.

DECORATING

1. Cut three 3-inch (7.6 cm) pieces of chenille stem. Thread each stem through a hole in the paper and metal.

2. Twist the ends of each stem together. Remove the clips.

3. Cut varying lengths of chenille stems. Twist them together to make designs.

4. Weave your designs through the holes in the front cover. You can change the designs anytime you want!

TIP

When you run out of paper in your notebook, just cut more sheets and undo the chenille stems to add them.

17

SHEET METAL JAR

CONSTRUCT A SECRET TRINKET TRAY!

MATERIALS

- hot glue gun & glue sticks
- 2 4" (10.2 cm) round duct caps
- 4" (10.2 cm) flex duct & sheet metal splice connector collar
- 14 to 19 ½" (1.3 cm) ceramic disc magnets
- 3" (7.6 cm) round steel gas vent tee cap
- ruler
- marker
- large nail
- hammer
- 16-gauge wire, 16" (40.6 cm) long
- 10 to 15 hex nuts

EASY

GLUING THE BASE + MAGNETS

1 Put on a face mask. Glue one duct cap on one end of the connector collar. Let the glue dry.

2 Glue four magnets on the tee cap's rim. Space them evenly. Let the glue dry.

MAKING THE LID + HANDLE

1 Lay the other duct cap on your work surface. Measure ½ inch (1.3 cm) in from the edge. Make a small mark.

Continued on the next page.

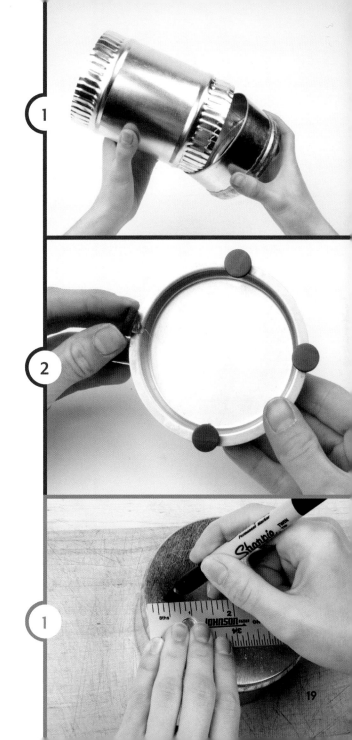

19

2 Make another mark ½ inch (1.3 cm) in from the opposite edge of the cap.

3 Use the nail and hammer to make a hole at each mark.

4 Push one end of the wire through each hole. Twist the ends together inside the lid. Flatten the ends against the inside of the cap.

5 Twist the wire loop on top of the cap once to make a smaller loop. This is the lid's handle.

FINISHING + FILLING

1   Put keys, money, or **trinkets** in the tee cap. Place it under the lid. The magnets will stick to the lid, making a hidden tray.

2   Fill the container with anything you like. Put the lid on the container.

3   Glue a magnet to each hex nut. Let the glue dry.

4   Use the hex nut magnets to decorate the outside of the container. Rearrange the design whenever you like!

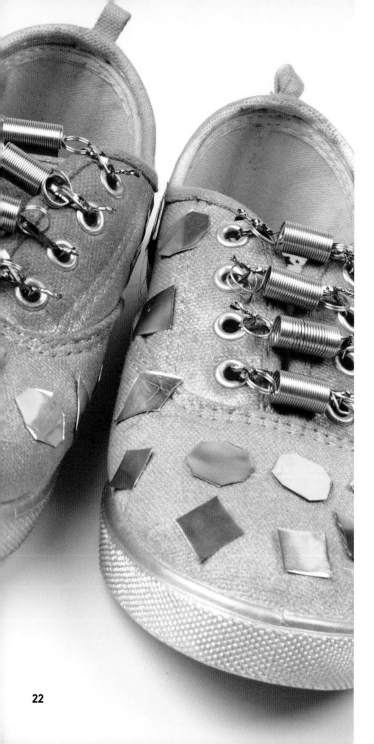

SHINY SHOES

ADD A COOL METAL
LOOK TO YOUR SHOES!

MATERIALS

- newspaper
- canvas or cotton sneakers
- rubber gloves
- silver or gold spray paint
- clear sealer
- paintbrush
- metal extension springs
- wire cutters
- needle-nose pliers
- 16 twist ties
- marker
- copper & aluminum foil
- scissors
- hot glue gun & glue sticks

INTERMEDIATE

PAINTING THE SHOES

1 Lay newspaper outside or in a well-**ventilated** area. Remove the laces from the sneakers. Place the shoes on the newspaper. Put on the face mask and gloves. Spray paint the sneakers. Let the paint dry.

2 Paint clear sealer on the outer sole of the sneaker. Let it dry.

Continued on the next page.

ATTACHING THE SPRINGS

1 Cut each spring in half with the wire cutters.

2 Use pliers to pull one or two coils out from each cut end.

3 Use the twist ties to attach a spring to each pair of **eyelets**. Trim the ends of the twist ties.

DECORATING

1 Draw shapes on the copper and aluminum foil. Cut them out.

2 Hot glue the shapes onto the shoes. Carefully press each shape to mold it to the shoe. Let the glue dry.

3 Your shimmering metallic shoes are ready to wear! The springs should stretch, allowing you to slip your feet into the shoes.

TIP
If your metallic shapes become dirty or torn, pluck them off! Glue on new shapes whenever you like.

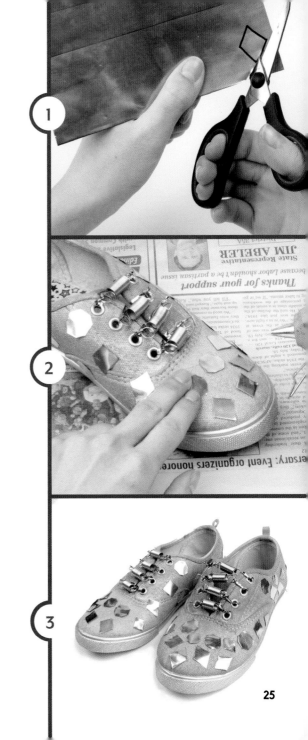

MILKY WAY METAL
MURAL

CREATE A SPARKLING METAL GALAXY!

MATERIALS

- thick cotton gloves with a rubber coating
- tin snips
- piece of copper sheet metal
- hammer
- large nail
- ruler
- 2 large, old towels
- rubber gloves
- large bowl
- measuring cup
- white vinegar
- spoon
- salt
- old rag
- clear spray adhesive
- glitter
- 1 to 2 aluminum baking pans
- marker
- several round tubs or cans
- scissors
- acrylic paint
- paintbrushes
- wire cutters
- flat copper wire
- needle-nose pliers
- metal glue
- galvanized wire

CUTTING + HAMMERING HOLES

1 Put on the thick gloves and safety goggles. Use tin snips to cut the copper sheet into the shape you want.

2 Lay the copper sheet on your work surface. Decide which edge will be the top of your **mural**. Use the hammer and nail to make a hole near each top corner. Make the holes about ¼ inch (0.6 cm) from the edges.

3 Decide where you want a **3-D** planet to be. Make a hole in that spot with the hammer and nail.

Continued on the next page.

27

MAKING + APPLYING THE PATINA MIXTURE

1 Fold each towel a couple times. **Stack** them on top of each other on your work surface. Set the copper on top of the towels. Take off the thick gloves.

2 Put on rubber gloves. Put about 2 cups of white vinegar in a bowl. Add a heaping spoonful of salt. Stir the mixture until it's cloudy.

3 Submerge a rag in the mixture. Lightly wring it out over the bowl.

4 Hold the rag over the copper. Wring it out again. Let the mixture drip and **splatter** on the copper.

5 Sprinkle salt over the copper. Use a large spoonful of salt, but sprinkle it evenly. Do not create piles of salt. Let it dry overnight.

6 When dry, parts of the copper should have a greenish **patina**. If this doesn't work the first time, repeat steps 2 through 5.

SEALING + DECORATING

1 Put on the face mask. Spray the copper with a thick layer of clear adhesive. While it is wet, sprinkle pinches of glitter to look like stars. Let it dry.

2 Trace circles on the baking pans. Make them different sizes. Cut them out. These will be planets and moons.

Continued on the next page.

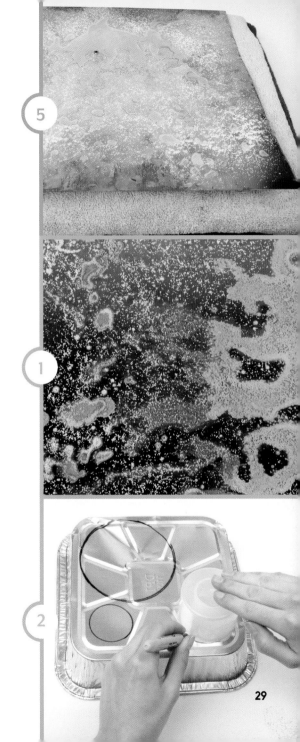

29

3 Paint and decorate your planets. Wrinkle some of them. Glue glitter to others. Get creative!

4 Cut a 5-inch (12.7 cm) piece of copper wire. Wrap it around a marker to make a coil. Push one end through the hole for your **3-D** planet. Using the pliers, bend this end behind the **mural** to secure. Bend the other end flat.

5 Put on the face mask. Glue one planet to the flat end of the coil. Your 3-D planet should spring to life! Glue the other planets and moons to the background.

6 Cut a piece of **galvanized** wire a few inches longer than the top edge of the mural. Push the wire ends through the corner holes. Twist the ends so they don't slide out.

7 Hang up your shining metal space mural!

GLOSSARY

3-D – having three dimensions, such as length, width, and height.

DANGEROUS – able or likely to cause harm or injury.

EYELET – a small hole for a lace or rope.

GALVANIZED – steel or iron coated with a layer of zinc to keep it from rusting.

INSERT – to stick something into something else.

MURAL – a large piece of art that is often painted on a wall or ceiling.

PATINA – a thin green layer that forms on copper and bronze when they are exposed to the air for a long time.

PERMISSION – when a person in charge says it is okay to do something.

SPLATTER – to be thrown or scattered around.

STACK – to arrange things in a pile.

TRINKET – a small item of little value.

VENTILATE – to allow fresh air to enter and move through a room.

Websites

To learn more about Cool Industrial Arts, visit **booklinks.abdopublishing.com**. These links are routinely monitored and updated to provide the most current information available.

INDEX